HOLY WEEK

ACTIVITY BOOK FOR LATTER-DAY SAINTS

ABOUT THIS BOOK

This book is a great resource for families to learn more about the final week of the life of our Savior. The book layout follows each day of Holy Week, beginning with Palm Sunday. Each day has a page explaining what happened on that particular day and scripture references to read as a family, if so desired.

The chronology of the final week of Christ's life is somewhat unclear, as the gospel accounts differ. However, this should not take away from the learning activities provided to help children and youth learn more about the most important week in history. Enjoy the journey through Holy Week!

THIS BOOK BELONGS TO:

_____

HOW MUCH DO YOU KNOW ABOUT HOLY WEEK?

See how much you already know about Holy Week. Match each picture to the corresponding words that tell of the final week of the life of Christ.

Palm Sunday - Joyful entrance to Jerusalem

Monday - Jesus cleanses the temple

Tuesday & Wednesday - Teaching in Jerusalem

Thursday - Passover & Ordinance of sacrament

Thursday - Garden of Gethsemane

Friday - Jesus is Crucified

Saturday - Christ's body in the tomb

Sunday - Jesus Christ is resurrected & appears to Mary & apostles

WHAT IS HOLY WEEK?

Holy week is celebrated by Christians around the world. It begins the Sunday before Easter Sunday and it is a time to remember the last week of the life of Jesus Christ, including the Atonement & Resurrection.

SUNDAY MONDAY  TUESDAY WEDNESDAY

The Sunday before Easter Sunday is called Palm Sunday & it celebrates Jesus' triumphal entry to Jerusalem. People took branches of palm trees to greet Jesus & cried, "Hosanna."

Jesus cleansed the temple by commanding the merchants and moneychangers to leave. The temple was to be a place of worship not a place of business. He healed sick at temple.

Jesus taught the multitudes many important parables, such as the ten virgins and the talents.

Judas Iscariot agreed to betray Jesus for thirty pieces of silver. Jesus may have done more teaching.

THURSDAY FRIDAY  SATURDAY SUNDAY

Jesus celebrated Passover. He had Last Supper with His apostles and introduced the sacrament. He performed Atonement in the Garden of Gethsemane. He was betrayed by Judas Iscariot and arrested.

Jesus was taken to Pilate and the multitude wanted Him crucified. He was scourged, mocked, spit upon, and crucified on a cross. He died. He is placed in a tomb.

Jesus' body lay in a tomb. His Spirit goes to the Spirit World.

Jesus' tomb is found empty. He is risen! He appears to Mary Magdalene, the disciples, and others.

PALM SUNDAY

The Sunday before Easter Sunday is called Palm Sunday & it celebrates Jesus' triumphal entry to Jerusalem. People took branches of palm trees to greet Jesus & cried, "Hosanna." Read Matthew 21:1-11 & Luke 19:29-44. Color pictures below that teach about this special day.

WHAT WAS THE MEANING BEHIND THE PALM BRANCHES?

Palms symbolize peace and victory. In Jesus' time, it was custom to lay down palm branches in front of people who were owed a great deal of respect. Read John 12:12-13.

WHY DID THE PEOPLE SPREAD THEIR CLOTHING ON THE GROUND?

Laying clothing on the ground had the same meaning as laying down the palm branches, it was a sign of respect. People not only placed palm branches on the ground, but clothing as Jesus entered Jerusalem. See Matthew 21:8.

IT WAS FORETOLD CHRIST WOULD ENTER JERUSALEM RIDING ON A DONKEY.

The Old Testament foretold Jesus entering Jerusalem riding on a donkey. Read Zechariah 9:9.

HOSANNA!

WHAT DOES "HOSANNA" MEAN?

The word *hosanna* is Hebrew and is a plea for salvation and means "save now, we pray." The multitude cried "Hosanna" as Jesus entered Jerusalem. See Matthew 21:9. Saying "Hosanna" reminds us that Jesus saved us by performing the Atonement, which allows us to repent and return back to live with Heavenly Father someday.

On the Palm leaf below, write or draw blessings you have in your life because of Heavenly Father & Jesus.

THINGS GOD HAS BLESSED ME WITH

WHAT IS THE HOSANNA SHOUT?

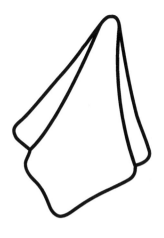

Just as the multitude waved palm branches as Christ entered Jerusalem, Latter-day Saints waive white handkerchiefs above their heads as a sacred tribute to Heavenly Father & Jesus.

The handkerchief is grabbed by the corner and waved above the head. If you don't have a handkerchief, you can wave your hand above your head. While waving your handkerchief, you say:

Hosanna, Hosanna, Hosanna to God and the Lamb.
Hosanna, Hosanna, Hosanna to God and the Lamb.
Hosanna, Hosanna, Hosanna to God and the Lamb.
Amen, Amen, and Amen.

WHEN DO WE DO THE HOSANNA SHOUT?

On joyous occasions, we say the Hosanna Shout. The Mormon pioneers waved their handkerchiefs when they entered the Salt Lake valley after their long journey.

At each temple dedication, beginning with the Kirtland Temple in 1836, the Hosanna Shout has been given.

In April 2020, the Hosanna Shout was done during General Conference to celebrated 200 years since Joseph Smith's First Vision of the Father and the Son.

CLEANSING MONDAY

CLEANSING THE TEMPLE

In His final week, Jesus cleansed the temple by commanding the merchants and moneychangers to leave. The temple was to be a place of worship not a place of business. Read Mark 11:15-18; Matthew 21:12-15; Luke 19:45-48.

WHO WERE MONEYCHANGERS?

In Jesus' time, those going to the temple had to pay a temple tax (tithing) to help with the maintenance of the temple. It had to be paid with a special coin called a shekel. People had to visit a moneychanger to change their regular money to this special coin to pay the tithing. The moneychangers at the temple were often greedy and overcharged for their services.

WHY DID JESUS OVERTHROW THE TABLES OF THOSE SELLING DOVES AT TEMPLE?

Merchants sold animals to sacrifice at the temple. The poor often bought doves for their sacrifices. Many of the merchants overcharged for the doves & took advantage of those purchasing. Jesus saw them as thieves & threw them out of the temple. Read Mark 11:15.

WHAT HAPPENED AFTER JESUS CLEANSED THE TEMPLE?

After the temple was cleansed of the merchants and moneychangers, Jesus healed the lame and blind at the temple. Read Matthew 21:14.

OUR BODIES ARE TEMPLES. HOW CAN YOU SANCTIFY YOUR BODY SO THE HOLY GHOST CAN DWELL WITH YOU?

Color the pictures below of ways you can "cleanse" your body and have Spirit dwell with you.

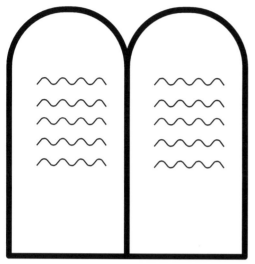

OBEY THE COMMANDMENTS

REPENT WHEN YOU MAKE A MISTAKE

BE BAPTIZED & KEEP BAPTISIMAL COVENANTS

PARTAKE OF THE SACRAMENT EACH WEEK & RENEW BAPTISIMAL COVENANTS

READ SCRIPTURES, PRAY, BE KIND

HOLY MONDAY WORD SEARCH

Find the hidden words below relating to Holy Monday including Jesus cleansing the temple, healing at temple, and the story of Jesus and withered fig tree.

```
E  E  T  F  M  R  E  B  H  Y  R  X
H  Y  E  S  F  S  V  Y  T  E  N  T
G  G  M  X  N  M  M  S  C  F  A  U
I  B  M  A  S  S  O  S  X  I  M  L
A  T  E  M  P  L  E  N  G  G  O  G
T  L  R  X  H  V  G  L  E  G  N  Y
C  D  C  U  O  L  C  F  Y  Y  D  I
O  L  H  D  Y  U  H  J  A  E  A  F
I  U  A  Q  K  Z  J  R  E  V  Y  U
N  J  N  Y  N  V  X  Q  M  S  C  U
Q  P  T  Q  I  G  O  G  P  A  U  Y
K  S  S  D  H  N  Q  X  O  S  C  S
```

TEMPLE	MERCHANTS	MONEY
DOVES	COIN	CLEANSE
JESUS	HEAL	FIG
MONDAY		

WHAT WAS THE MEANING OF THE STORY OF THE WITHERED FIG TREE?

Read Matthew 21:18-22 and Mark 11:12-14 and discuss with your family the meaning of the story of the withered fig tree.

HELP THE SICK MAN FIND JESUS

Help the sick man find the correct path to Jesus at the temple so he can be healed.

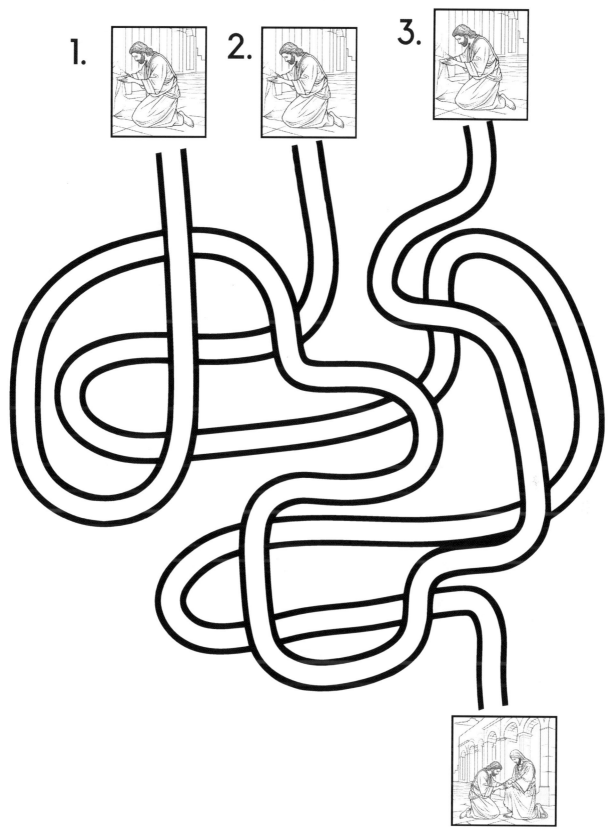

TEACHING TUESDAY

During the last week of His life, the Savior taught many of His most well-known parables. Color the pictures and read about the parables below & discuss with your family. See Matthew 13:10-13.

WHAT IS A PARABLE?

Jesus was a master teacher. He didn't just clearly state His message, but He taught His message through stories. He left it up to the listeners to figure out what the stories meant and how to apply to their own lives.

PARABLE OF THE TEN VIRIGINS

Ten virgins were waiting to meet the bridegroom. Five were wise and filled their lamps with oil. Five were foolish and didn't put oil in their lamps. The bridegroom came at midnight and the five virgins that didn't have oil couldn't light their lamps to go into the wedding and were shut out. Read Matthew 25:1-13.

We are like the ten virgins. We are waiting for Jesus to come again (the bridegroom). We must add oil to our lamps. That oil is our faith and testimonies. Our testimony is gained through our good works, obedience to commandments, and dedication to our covenants. It isn't something that can be shared, as spiritual preparation must be done by each individual. Write things you can do to increase your faith and testimony of drops of oil below.

PARABLE OF THE TEN TALENTS

A master gave one of his servants five talents, another two talents, and the third he gave one talent. The first two servants doubled their talents when they returned and were told by the master they would be "ruler over many things" and enter the "joy of the Lord." However, the third servant buried his talent. The master called him "wicked and slothful" and the servant's talent was taken from him and given to him that had ten talents. Read Matthew 25:14-30.

The Lord gave each of us talents that He wants us to add upon these talents as well as gain more. What are your talents? Write your talents on coins below. How can you use them to build God's kingdom?

CAN YOU SPOT THE DIFFERENCES?

Compare the top and bottom picture and spot seven differences between the two pictures and circle.

The Parable of the Ten Virgins teaches us we must nourish our faith and testimonies, even if they just start as a tiny seeds as Alma teaches (Alma 32:28–43). Plants get nourishment from water, sunlight, good soil, and care. How can you care for your testimony? Color the picture below.

MY TESTIMONY GROWS AS I NOURISH IT

WHEN WE SERVE OTHERS, WE SERVE GOD

Read Matthew 25:31-46. Jesus teaches us in these verses that when we serve those in need--the poor, sick, needy--we are serving Him. Think of someone you can serve this week and draw a picture or write about what you are going to do in the box below.

SPY WEDNESDAY

Judas Iscariot was one of Jesus' apostles. For the small amount of 30 pieces of silver, he told the chief priests (who wanted to put Jesus to death) he would deliver Jesus to them. Judas was then a "spy" among the apostles and he began waiting for the opportunity to betray the Savior. Read Matthew 26:14-16.

HOW MUCH DO YOU KNOW ABOUT JUDAS ISCARIOT?

Match the picture to the corresponding fact about Judas Iscariot.

Judas was the treasurer for the 12 apostles & kept the money bag. However, he is called a "thief" as he used some of the money for the ministry for himself. See John 12:6 and 13:29.

When Judas heard Jesus was condemned to death, he realized the horrible thing he had done. He threw the 30 pieces of silver in the temple and went and killed himself. See Matthew 27:5.

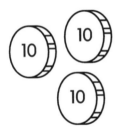

When Mary Magdalene washed Jesus' feet with her hair and an expensive ointment, Judas was upset. He said that money could have been given to the poor. However, he did not care for the poor, he just was greedy. See John 12:6.

Judas went to the chief priests who wanted to condemn Jesus and agreed to deliver Jesus to them for the small amount of 30 pieces of silver. 30 pieces of silver was the price of the life of a slave at that time. See Exodus 21:32.

Judas led the chief priests to Gethsemane and showed them who Jesus was by kissing Jesus. Jesus was then taken away to be sentenced to His death. See Matthew 26:48.

LOVE GOD & OTHERS

Jesus may have also done more teaching on the final Wednesday before his death. The two great commandments Jesus taught are to love God with all your heart and to love your neighbor. Fill in the missing words from John 13:34 below.

"A new _____I give unto you, That ye _____one another; as I have ____you, that ye also love one _____."

Use the words below to fill in the blanks above.

another love commandment loved

Write the names of some of your "neighbors" you can love on hearts below.

FIND THE HIDDEN PICTURES

Find the hidden pictures listed below in the picture of Christ teaching the people.
Color or circle them when you find them.

HOLY THURSDAY
THE LAST SUPPER AND GARDEN OF GETHSEMANE

The evening before Jesus was to be crucified, Jesus sat down with His apostles to have a meal together, which we now call the Last Supper. This meal was during the Jewish holiday of Passover. Jesus instituted the sacrament using bread and wine. That night, Jesus went to the Garden of Gethsemane to begin His atoning sacrifice.

WHAT IS PASSOVER?

The Feast of the Passover began to help the children of Israel remember the miracle of God delivering them from the bondage of Pharoah in Egypt. The Israelite families each sacrificed a lamb and wiped the blood of the lamb on their doorways. Those who did this were saved from the plague of death of their firstborn son. This finally convinced Pharoah to let the Israelite leave Egypt. See Exodus 12.

WHAT WAS THE LAST SUPPER?

The evening of the Last Supper, the Savior washed His apostles feet. He foretold that Judas would betray Him. Jesus then taught the ordinance of the sacrament. He broke bread as a symbol of His body. Then he blessed a cup of wine and told it was to remind them of His blood. See Mark 14:12-25.

WHAT HAPPENED IN GETHSEMANE?

After the Last Supper, Jesus went with eleven of his apostles to Gethsemane. Gethsemane was an olive tree grove where olives were harvested and crushed to make olive oil. It was here that Christ bled from every pore and paid for all our sins and sorrows. Judas led those seeking to arrest Jesus to the garden and betrayed Him with a kiss. See Matthew 26:36-46.

THE SACRAMENT HELPS ME REMEMBER JESUS

Each week when you partake of the sacrament, you can remember Jesus and His sacrifice and how we can be more like Him. Color the ways to think of Him below.

BIBLE

I can think of Jesus by reading a scripture about Him

I can think of Jesus by reading a sacrament hymn or primary song about Him

I can think of Jesus by looking at a picture of Him

I CAN REPENT

No one is perfect. The only perfect person that ever lived was Jesus. Repentance brings us joy. We can repent because Jesus atoned for our sins in the Garden of Gethsemane. Color the steps of repentance below.

acknowledge what you did was wrong

I'M SORRY

say "i'm sorry" & fix what you did

ask heavenly father for forgiveness

receive peace & forgiveness & try your best not to repeat mistake

HOLY THURSDAY WORD SEARCH

Find the hidden words below relating to Passover, the Last Supper, and the Atonement in the Garden of Gethsemane. Write your name below on the blank line. Jesus loves you!

```
M  O  A  T  O  N  E  M  E  N  T  Y
Z  N  N  B  Z  L  P  V  W  Z  S  A
N  N  P  J  E  N  G  C  D  W  X  S
Y  Y  A  J  H  T  F  I  X  Z  E  A
G  R  S  G  S  V  R  T  I  B  D  C
X  O  S  A  U  I  C  A  X  L  U  R
Z  M  O  R  F  A  T  R  Y  O  X  A
M  A  V  D  F  B  R  C  U  O  M  M
Q  M  E  E  H  P  C  R  D  Q  E
K  E  R  N  R  T  D  R  Z  L  N
L  I  B  O  D  Y  D  P  W  U  A  T
R  R  R  E  M  E  M  B  E  R  P  T
```

PASSOVER	REMEMBER	SACRAMENT
BLOOD	BODY	SUFFER
GARDEN	ATONEMENT	BETRAY

JESUS SUFFERED
BECAUSE HE LOVES
ME, _____.

JESUS KNOWS AND LOVES YOU

Jesus suffered in the Garden of Gethsemane because He loves you! He felt all your sins and wanted you to have a way to repent so you could return to live with Heavenly Father someday. Draw a picture of yourself below and write your name in the blank below the picture frame.

JESUS SUFFERED BECAUSE HE LOVES ME, _____.

I CAN PRAY & ASK HEAVENLY FATHER FOR HELP

In Luke 22:41–43, when Jesus was praying in the Garden of Gethsemane an angel was sent to help strengthen Him. You can pray to Heavenly Father for help & strength, too. Write or draw things you can pray about below.

Things I Can Pray For

GOOD FRIDAY
JESUS IS CRUCIFIED

The Friday before His death, Jesus was brought to trial before Pontius Pilate. Pilate didn't think Jesus was guilty of any crime, but the crowd wanted to crucify Jesus. Jesus was treated horribly before being crucified. He suffered on the cross and died. See Matthew 27.

WHY IS IT CALLED GOOD FRIDAY?

If we are remembering Jesus being crucified on this Friday, why is it called "good?" The word good in this context is meant to mean holy. Because Christ was resurrected, we all will be resurrected again someday, too. Because of His atonement we can repent of our sins. That is why we call this day "good" or holy.

WHO WAS PONTIUS PILATE?

Pilate was the governor of the Roman providence of Judea. He presided over the trial of Jesus. Pilate's wife told Pilate to "Have thou nothing to do with that just man." See Matthew 27:19. Pilate asked the crowd if he should release Jesus, but they wanted to crucify Him. Pilate washed his hands and said he was "innocent of the blood of this just person." Jesus was then released to be crucified.

WHAT HAPPENED TO JESUS BEFORE HE WAS CRUCIFIED?

Jesus was scourged (severe whipping), stripped of clothing and a scarlet robe placed on Him, a crown of thorns placed on his head, a reed placed in His right hand. He was mocked and spit upon and hit in the head.

WHERE WAS GOLGOTHA?

Golgotha means "skull" and it is where Jesus was crucified and nailed to a cross. Two other thieves were also crucified. Jesus asked Heavenly Father to forgive the soldiers that crucified Him, as they didn't know He was the Savior. After the Savior died, the earth quaked and a veil at the temple was torn in two.

WHAT HAPPENED IN THE AMERICAS WHEN JESUS WAS CRUCIFIED?

There were tempests, earthquakes, and fires and three days of darkness. See 3 Nephi 8.

CRACK THE CODE

An unlikely testimony from a Roman Solider is recorded in the Bible. He testified that Jesus was the Savior. Use the key below to find out what the soldier said. See Matthew 27:54.

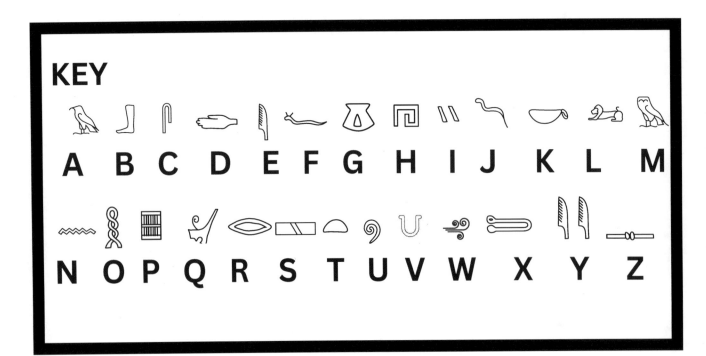

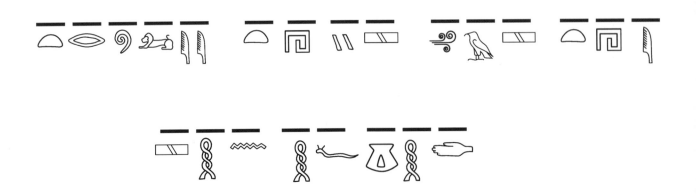

SATURDAY IN THE TOMB

Jesus' followers were mourning His loss the day after His death. He was caringly prepared and placed in a tomb. See Matthew 27:55–61.

WHAT HAPPENED TO JESUS' BODY AFTER HE DIED?

Friday after Jesus died, Joseph of Arimathea went to Pilate and pleaded for His body. Joseph was a follower of Jesus but also a wealthy, prominent member of the Sanhedrin (group of religious leaders that wanted Jesus crucified). Joseph risked his reputation asking for Christ's body. Joseph wrapped Jesus' body in linen cloth and put Jesus' body in his own tomb as they needed to hurry to be finished with preparations before the Jewish Sabbath (Saturday).

WHERE DID JESUS' SPIRIT GO AFTER HE DIED?

Jesus' physical body had died but His spirit still lived. Jesus went to the spirit world and was greeted by many great and faithful spirits who had lived on Earth. Many had died long ago and were ready to be resurrected. There were also spirits who had not heard of Christ's gospel that needed to be preached to. See 1 Peter 3:18-18 and D&C 138.

COMPLETE CROSSWORD PUZZLE BELOW

DOWN

1-Which day of the week is the Jewish sabbath?

2-The last name of the Governor of Judea who washed his hands clean before letting the multitude crucify Jesus.

ACROSS

3-After He died, Jesus' body was placed in what?

4-In the Garden of Gethsemane, Jesus bled from every ____.

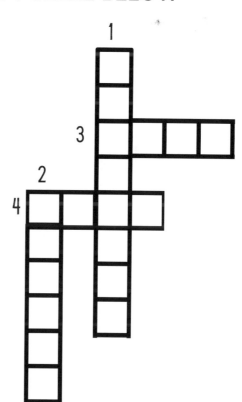

WRITE A NOTE TO JESUS

On the note below, write Jesus a thank you card for all He has done for you. You can even add a picture!

THANK YOU!

To: _____

From: _____

EASTER SUNDAY
JESUS IS RESURRECTED

Mary Magdalene was surprised to find Jesus' tomb empty on Sunday morning when she visited. He was not there and He had risen! Read John 20:1-21 & Matthew 28:1-10.

WHAT DID MARY FIND WHEN SHE VISITED THE TOMB?

Mary Magdalene went on Sunday morning to see the tomb. She was visited by an angel and the angel rolled back the stone to the empty tomb and told her Jesus was not there because he had risen. The angel told Mary to go tell the disciples.

WHO DID THE RESURRECTED JESUS APPEAR TO ON SUNDAY?

Jesus appeared first to Mary Magdalene (John 20:16), then to other women (Matthew 28:9), two disciples (Luke 24:13-32), Simon Peter (Luke 24:34), the apostles and small group of others (Luke 24:33).

WHO WILL BE RESURRECTED?

Jesus was resurrected. Because of Him, every person who has lived on this earth will be resurrected. Complete the maze below. Start at headstone & finish with the resurrected body.

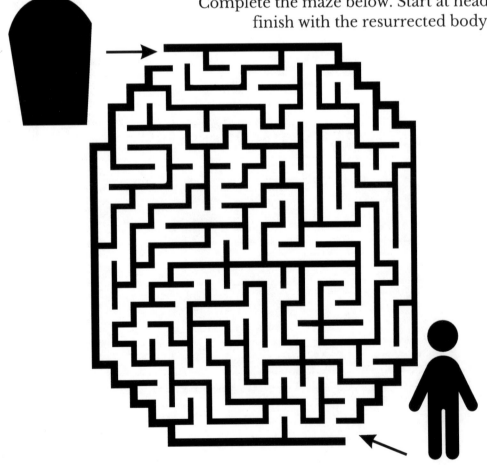

JESUS CHRIST VISITED THE NEPHITES

In 3 Nephi 11, Jesus Christ showed himself to the people of Nephi. He let them feel the nail prints in his hands and feet. Draw a picture of what you think this looked like.

TIMELINE OF EVENTS LEADING TO THE RESURRECTED CHRIST VISITING THE NEPHITES

In 3 Nephi chapters 8 & 9, we learn about the events that occurred to the Nephites after the Savior was resurrected. Match the description to it's picture below.

Great doubting among people that Christ would come

Great storm, earthquakes, fires, cities sunk, wicked destroyed

Great darkness for three days

The people hear a voice three times & finally understand it is God introducing his son & Jesus christ descends. The people feel his nail prints

Jesus teaches about baptism

EASTER WORD SEARCH

Find the hidden words in the word search below. Color the "He Lives!"
lettering.

```
N M G L O R I O U S T A
E N D T O M B C Y E D P
G Q K T S S G E S S G E
H Q E A S T E R X M A W
J I C K T S S K R O P K
I L B G R A T I T U D E
C F F V K U L K P D R M
V X I Z U W Y G S F B P
U T Q L V Y I C E V I T
P M I R A C U L O U S Y
X P S U N D A Y U W H K
D L I V E S A V I O R C
```

EASTER	SUNDAY	GLORIOUS
LIVES	SAVIOR	GRATITUDE
MIRACULOUS	EMPTY	TOMB

SYMBOL OF EASTER EGGS

Eggs have been a symbol of Easter for hundreds of years. Eggs represent the empty tomb from which Jesus was resurrected. The egg is a reminder that we will all be resurrected some day. Hunting for eggs is a reminder that we must seek God and Christ in our lives.

Color the eggs below.

MY TESTIMONY

Below write your testimony of Jesus Christ and His Gospel. You can also write anything new you learned about Holy Week.

_____

_____

_____

_____

_____

_____

_____

_____

_____

_____

_____

_____

_____

_____

_____

_____

_____

_____

_____

_____

_____

_____

_____

_____

_____

IF YOU ENJOYED THIS BOOK, MAKE SURE TO LEAVE A REVIEW.

CHECK OUT OUR OTHER BOOKS.

FOLLOW US ONLINE!

@LATTER.DAY.DESIGNS

LATTER-DAY DESIGNS

Made in the USA
Columbia, SC
12 April 2025

56498152R00024